BASIC MANNERS

The Child's World®

Published by The Child's World®
1980 Lookout Drive • Mankato, MN 56003-1705
800-599-READ • www.childsworld.com

Acknowledgments
The Child's World®: Mary Berendes, Publishing Director
The Design Lab: Design and production
Red Line Editorial: Editorial direction

ISBN 9781614732235
LCCN 2012932440

Printed in the United States of America
Mankato, MN
July 2012
PA02126

ABOUT THE AUTHOR

Ann Ingalls writes stories and poems for people of all ages as well as resource materials for parents and teachers. She was a teacher for many years and enjoys working with children. When she isn't writing, she enjoys spending time with her family and friends, traveling, reading, knitting, and playing with her cats.

ABOUT THE ILLUSTRATOR

Ronnie Rooney took art classes constantly as a child. She was always drawing and painting at her mom's kitchen table. She got her BFA in painting from the University of Massachusetts at Amherst and her MFA in Illustration from Savannah College of Art and Design in Savannah, Georgia. She now lives and works in Fort Lewis, Washington. Her plan is to pass her love of art and sports on to her two young children.

CONTENTS

Basic Manners

Do you want to have friends? Do you want to feel good about yourself? Do you want to be **welcome** at the places you go?

The best way to do this is to learn good manners. Good manners matter. Watch the way people treat each other. Think about how you like to be treated. Someone else may act like a goon. But you don't need to act that way, too.

Learn and practice good manners now. You will have them for the rest of your life.

Greet Others

When someone comes to your house, say, "Hello." Put on a happy face. Shake hands if you like. This makes guests feel welcome. Do not shake too hard. You will rattle their brains!

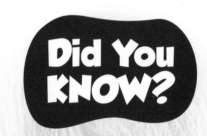

Did You KNOW?

In China, smiling at someone you don't know well is thought to be rude.

Take Turns

Be quiet and listen when someone else is speaking. Wait your turn to speak. Ask a question when the person is done talking. Do not raise your hand and call out, "My turn, my turn!" or, "Me, me, me!"

Remember, there are enough seats on the roller coaster for everyone. You do not need to push in line. Don't be a bulldozer and knock people off their feet. It will not make you anyone's best friend.

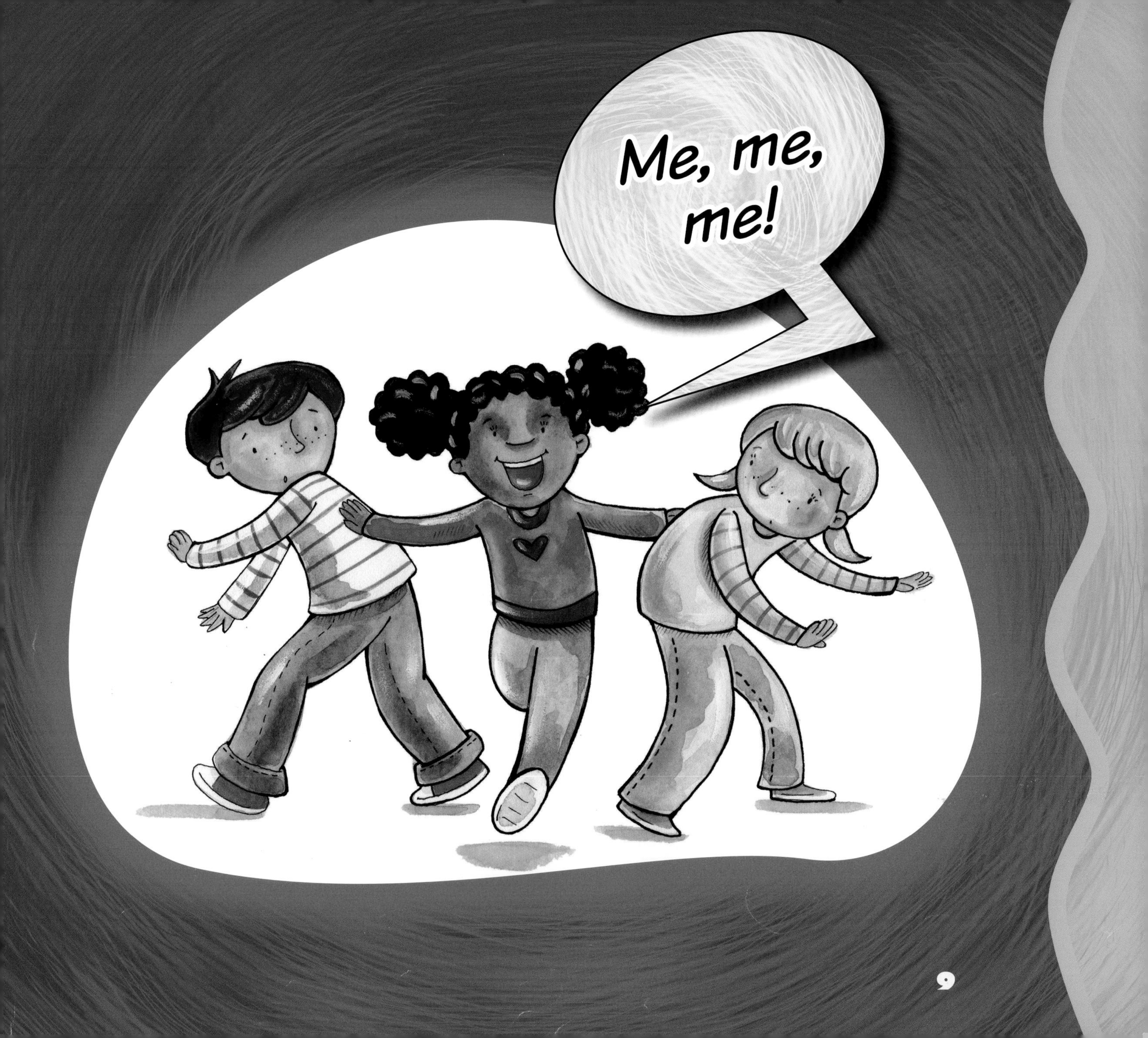
Me, me, me!

Tell the Truth

People trust others who tell the truth. Did you eat the last piece of pie that Mom was saving for Dad? Tell the truth. If you made a face at your baby sister and made her cry, just tell the truth.

Sometimes saying what you think is not a great thing to do. Some things can hurt another person's feelings. Hearing that someone thinks you look or smell bad can hurt. No one likes to be called "stinky feet." It does not matter if that person really does have stinky feet. Keep those thoughts to yourself.

Be a Good Sport

Be **polite** after playing a game. It does not matter who won. Do not brag or show off. Be kind. If you lose, do not sulk or get mad. Do not throw the playing cards all over the room. Not everyone can win at the same time.

Be a good sport. Tell the other players, "Good game!" This can be hard, but you can do it.

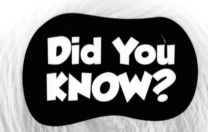

Did You KNOW?

Team players and coaches do not always show good manners. You may see your sports hero throw a fit or start a fight. That is not nice!

13

14

Be Gracious

If someone says, "Good job," be sure to say, "Thank you." This shows you are a **gracious** person. And don't put someone else down or point out his or her mistakes. It is never good if someone cries because of something you said. Say, "I'm sorry."

When someone thanks you, say, "You're welcome." Once is enough. You don't want to sound like a broken record.

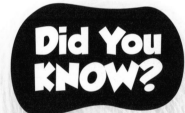

Did You KNOW?

In South America, people kiss on the cheek. Sometimes they kiss on both cheeks. They do this to say "hello."

Going In, Out, Up, or Down

Let people off the elevator first. Or let them on an escalator before you get on. It's best not to push or shove your way on.

If someone is going out of a door and you are going in, let the other person go first. It is just the nice thing to do.

Open the door for others. Let older folks or families with young children go first. Parents have their hands full with diaper bags, strollers, and toys.

If you walk through a door first, don't let it slam on the person behind you. Hold it until that person can grab it.

If someone holds the door for you, remember to say, "Thank you!"

17

Every Family Is Different

Each family has their own ways of doing things. They may be different from what you are used to. People come from different countries and **cultures**. You might eat spaghetti on Sundays. Your friend might eat fried rice, pickled beets, or strudel. If you are eating dinner at a friend's house, always give new foods a try. You might like them. Fried frog legs or pickled pig's feet might be yummy!

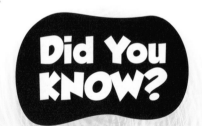

Did You KNOW?

Japanese children bow when they go to someone's house for dinner.

A Bit More Polite

Here is one last bit of **advice**. Do not be a slob. Clean up after yourself! When you finger paint at school, do not wear it home. When you eat dinner at a friend's home, take your dishes to the sink.

Good manners make everyone feel good. They help us make friends and solve problems.

You will surely think of other ways to use your manners. Practice them and you might be the best-liked kid in town.

Quick QUIZ

Put your new basic manners in action with this pop quiz! Will you make the polite move?

When you are waiting in line, the best thing to do is:

a. shove others out of the way.

b. wait until the person in front of you has had her turn.

c. yell, "Get out of my way!"

d. throw yourself down on the ground and have a fit.

When you are waiting for your turn to speak, the best thing to do is:

a. give the person speaking your full attention.

b. say, "You've talked long enough. It's my turn."

c. wait until they are done talking before you ask a question.

d. both A and C.

Calling someone names:

a. is never a good idea.

b. is all right as long as someone else does it first.

c. is fun. Do it whenever you like.

d. helps the person feel good.

When you walk through a door first:

a. let it slam on the person behind you.

b. push elderly people out of the way.

c. push families with young children out of the way.

d. do not let the door slam on the person behind you.

If you go to someone's home and they are eating food you have never eaten:

a. tell them you want a PB and J sandwich.

b. tell them your mother is a better cook.

c. order a pizza.

d. try the food that has been made.

When someone makes a mistake:

a. make sure everyone knows about it.

b. say, "I cannot believe you did such a silly thing."

c. laugh your head off.

d. tell them, "That's okay. We all make mistakes sometimes."

Please do not write in the book!

Glossary

advice (ad-VICE): To give advice is to say what someone should do. Her advice is to have good manners.

cultures (KUHL-churz): Cultures are the ways of life of different groups of people. People of different cultures eat different foods.

gracious (GRAY-shuss): To be gracious is to be kind and pleasant. It was gracious of her to say "thank you."

polite (puh-LITE): To be polite is to have good manners. It is polite to hold the door for others.

welcome (WEL-kuhm): People are welcome when a host feels glad to have them in his or her home. Paul felt welcome in Nancy's home.

Web Sites

Visit our Web site for links about basic manners:
childsworld.com/links

Note to Parents, Teachers, and Librarians: We routinely verify our Web links to make sure they are safe and active sites. So encourage your readers to check them out!

Books

Bridges, John, and Curtis, Bryan. *50 Things Every Young Gentleman Should Know.* Nashville, TN: Rutledge Hill Press, 2006.

Burstein, John. *Manners, Please!: Why It Pays to be Polite.* New York: Crabtree, 2011.

Eberly, Sheryl. *365 Manners Kids Should Know: Games, Activities, and Other Fun Ways to Help Children Learn Etiquette.* New York: Three Rivers Press, 2001.

Espeland, Pamela. *Dude, That's Rude!* Minneapolis, MN: Free Spirit Publishing, 2007.

Holyoke, Nancy. *A Smart Girl's Guide to Manners.* Middleton, WI: American Girl, 2005.

Index